Bot to Pot

by Anita Stasson

Consultant:
Beth Gambro
Reading Specialist
Yorkville, Illinois

Contents

Bot to Pot. 2

Key Words in the *-ot* Family 16

Index 16

About the Author. 16

Minneapolis, Minnesota

Bot to Pot

I see a red **bot**.

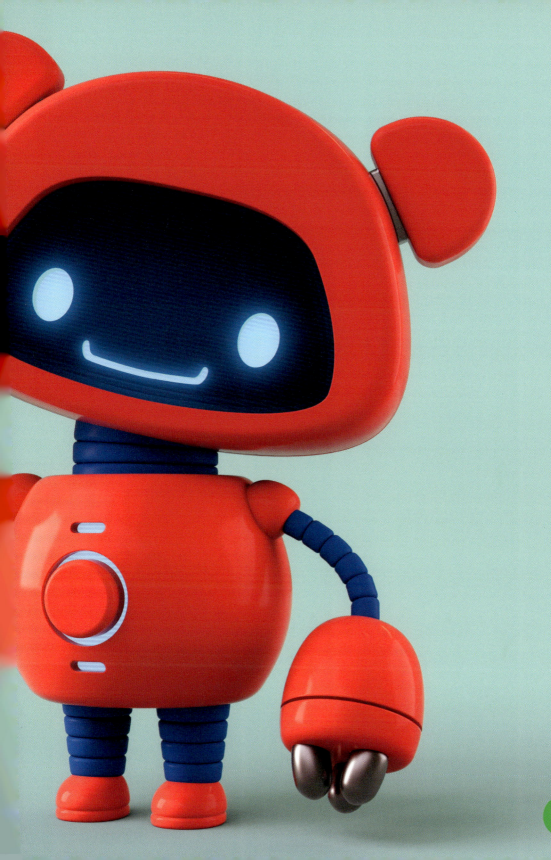

I see a wet **spot**.

I see a big **cot**.

I see a car **lot**.

I see a green **dot**.

I see a mail **slot**.

I see a clay **pot**.

Key Words in the -ot Family

bot   **cot**   **dot**   **lot**

pot   **slot**   **spot**

Other **-ot** Words: **got, hot, not, rot**

Index

bot 2
cot 7
dot 11
lot 9
pot 15
slot 12
spot 4

About the Author

Anita Stasson lives in Minnesota. She thinks rhyming is the bee's knees.

Teaching Tips

Before Reading
- ✔ Introduce rhyming words and the **–ot** word family to readers.
- ✔ Guide readers on a picture walk through the text by asking them to name the things shown.
- ✔ Discuss book structure by showing children where text will appear consistently on pages. Highlight the supportive pattern of the book.

During Reading
- ✔ Encourage readers to read with their finger and point to each word as it is read. Stop periodically to ask children to point to a specific word in the text.
- ✔ When encountering unknown words, prompt readers with encouraging cues such as:
  - **Does that word look like a word you already know?**
  - **Does it rhyme with another word you have already read?**

After Reading
- ✔ Write the key words on index cards.
  - **Have readers match them to pictures in the book.**
- ✔ Ask readers to identify their favorite page in the book. Have them read that page aloud.
- ✔ Choose an **–ot** word. Ask children to pick a word that rhymes with it.
- ✔ Ask children to create their own rhymes using **–ot** words. Encourage them to use the same pattern found in the book.